LEARNING WITH LE[TTS]
For six- to seven-year-o[lds]

Accident!

Story by Irene Yates
Activities by David Bell, Geoff Leyland,
Mick Seller and Irene Yates

Illustrations by Peter Joyce

People who live in Cherry Walk

For Lesley

Mark was playing with his new friend, Rose, at her house.

Rose's dad was due home from a trip.

'My dad's very important, you know!' Rose boasted.

Mark and Rose are playing pairs. Who has a pair of cards the same?

If Mark has four pairs of cards, how many cards does he have altogether? If Rose has three pairs of cards, how many cards does she have altogether?

What card games do you know? In which of them do you have to count or add up? Try to make up your own card game using numbers.

Everyone rushed outside to greet Rose's dad.

Mark peered through the windows.
Rose's dad certainly looked important

'Oh, Desmond darling!' said Rose's mum.

Rose's dad is wearing warm clothes for a cold day. Look at your clothes. Which are best for a hot day and which are best for a cold day? How are they different? What are they made of?

Make some warm squash. Pour it into four plastic containers with lids. Put the same amount in each one. Wrap each container in different material, such as a newspaper, a sock . . .

Leave the containers for ten minutes in a cold place. Taste the squash.
Which material was the best for keeping the squash warm?

Desmond-darling was so tired he had to go straight to bed.

'That's because he's been all over the world in an aeroplane,' Rose said, busily unwrapping her present.

Why is Rose's dad going to bed during the day?
What time is it?
Do you ever sleep during the day?
Do you know any people who work at night and sleep during the day?
What work do they do?

What's the earliest you have ever woken up?
What's the latest you have been to bed?

Draw two clocks like this and draw the hands on each to show the two times.

'He's been to America!' said Wesley.

'And Japan!' cried Charley.

'And Coventry!' shouted Rose.

Mark had never heard of Coventry. Desmond-darling must be extremely important!

Talk about places you have visited.
What is the longest journey you have ever made?
How did you travel?
How long did it take you?

How long does it take you to get to school?
How do you get there?

Which do you think is nearer to your home,
your school or the nearest sweet shop?
How can you check to make sure you are right?

Mark was jealous. He didn't want Rose's dad to be more important than his dad. Then he had an idea.

'That's nothing. My dad's a **spaceman**!'

The twins looked at him doubtfully.

'He is!' Mark said. 'He goes to the moon!'

Each night for a week, look out of the window just before bedtime.
Can you see the moon?
Which is best for moon-watching – a cloudy night or a clear night?

What shape is the moon?

Is it a full moon, a half moon, or a new moon?

It might be somewhere in between. It might be the other way round, like this!

Draw a picture of the moon each night.
Write the day of the week under each drawing.

Rose's eyes grew wider. 'The moon?'

'Cor!' said Wesley.

'I bet he's making it up,' said Charley.
'Let's go to his house and find out.'

Who thinks Mark is telling the truth? Why does Charley think he may be making it up? What do you think?

How can Charley find out whether it's a story or not when he gets to Mark's house?

What might happen when they get to Mark's house?

'I s'pose the moon's further away than Coventry,' Rose said in a disappointed little voice.

'It's further than everywhere,' said Charley. 'Nobody can go further than the moon.'

How many of these shapes can you find in the picture – squares, rectangles, triangles, circles?

If you have some gummed paper shapes find some triangles that are all the same size.
Draw a rectangle on a piece of paper.
See if you can cover the rectangle with the triangles.
Do they all fit exactly?
Are there any spaces?

You could do the same thing with gummed paper rectangles.

'Unless they go to Mars,' Wesley said.

'Does your dad go to Mars, Mark?'

Before Mark could answer, Boy appeared out of Mr Johnson's garden and started to bark at them.

Then he ran up the path and began to whine by the side gate.

What clues can you see in the picture which tell you that something is wrong?

Does Rose know what Boy wants?

How do animals let people know what they want?

Do you have a pet?
Can it tell you what it wants? How?

How do animals communicate with each other?

'Mr Johnson will go mad if he finds the dog in his garden,' Wesley said anxiously. 'What's the matter with him?'

'He wants to show us something, silly!' Rose shouted back as she ran after Boy.

Do you think Rose will catch up with Boy?
Guess who can run faster – Rose or Boy.

See how fast you can run.

Choose your starting and finishing line.
Ask a grown-up to count while you run.
Before you start, guess what number they
will count up to.

How good was your guess?

Now run again. Can you do it faster?
Guess what number they will count to this time.

Try doing this again with a friend as well.

'We'll get into terrible trouble!' Mark whispered. But the boys followed Rose all the same.

The birds were going mad in the aviary, flying from one perch to another.
Flap, flap, flap. Squawk, squawk, squawk.

See if you can sort the birds into their different colours. Draw a chart like this:

green yellow blue grey

Draw a picture for each bird in the right column. How many birds do you have in each column?

'Oh no! Look at the dog!' Charley cried.

'I'll get him!' shouted Wesley.
He crept up to the house, trying to stay low so that Mr Johnson wouldn't see him.

Look at the panes of glass in the back door.

How many rows are there?
How many panes of glass are there in each row?

How many panes are there altogether?

Suddenly Wesley shouted.

'It's Mr Johnson! He's lying on the floor! All in a heap! Fetch somebody quick.'

What can Wesley see through the window?

How might he feel?

How does he know something is wrong?

What different things could the children do next?

What is the best thing they could do?

Why?

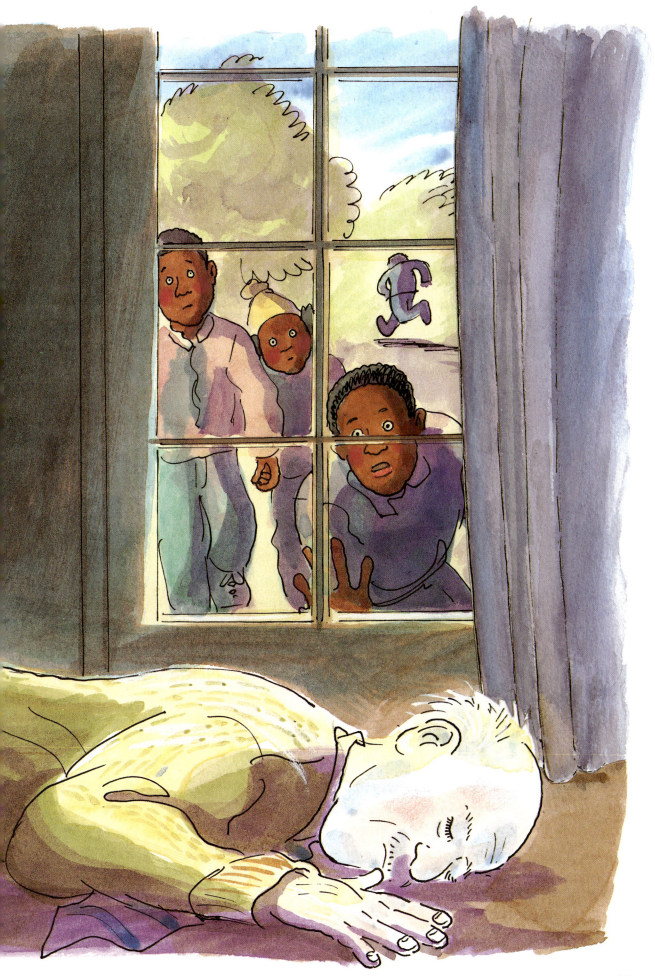

Mark's mum came running.
She had to find the spare key to the back door.

She shouted, 'Quick! One of you phone 999.
Tell them we need an ambulance.'

Ask mum or dad if you can look at their key ring.
Do you know what all the keys are for?
Try guessing the ones you don't know.
Do they have any unusual keys – maybe a very old one, or a plastic key card?

Put five similar keys into a bag and shake them.
Empty them on to a table.
Which door is each one for?
Are there any names or clues on the keys to help you?
Try your guesses out.
Were you right?

The ambulance came very quickly.
But it seemed like ages to the children.

Mark's dad came rushing down the street.

'Where's his space helmet?'
asked Wesley suspiciously.

'And why isn't he on the moon?' said Rose.

The children thought the time had passed slowly. If you have a watch that counts seconds, see if you can tell when ten seconds have gone by without looking at it. Get someone to look at the watch to see how close your guess is.

Now see if you can do the same thing with one minute.

'It's Mr Johnson, Dad.
I'll tell you all about it.
Why are you home early?' asked Mark.

'I've got some secret papers to look at, Mark.'

'You see,' Mark said proudly to the others.
'He's on a secret mission!'

Suppose Mark's dad really was a spaceman. Make up a secret adventure he might have had.

Divide a piece of paper into eight sections and make a comic strip of the adventure.

You will need to draw each thing that happens and write in speech bubbles.

Activity notes

Pages 2–3 This activity introduces your child to multiplication. Give them practice in adding groups of objects, eg 2 apples + 2 apples + 2 apples. At this stage children will just add the groups, but you can point out that they have three groups of two.

Pages 4–5 Here your child is investigating the idea of insulation. After you have both tasted the squash you can talk about the kind of material that seems to insulate best: is it the thickest, the softest . . . ?

Pages 6–7 Realising that not everybody shares the same time pattern of waking and sleeping can help reinforce understanding of the passage of time. Talking about the times when you regularly do things at home will help your child learn to tell the time.

Pages 8–9 Using simple comparisons can help your child estimate distances, eg does it take longer to get to school than to go into town? Ask them to explain their answer if they can. At this stage don't expect accuracy either about distances or time.

Pages 10–11 This activity encourages children to observe and record the moon and the way it changes, and is a first step in learning about our solar system.

Pages 12–13 These questions take the story several steps further than the words actually on the page and encourage reading between the lines, an important skill in reading.

Pages 14–15 Children can recognise common two-dimensional shapes from a very young age. They need to be able to explore the different features of these shapes. One of these is whether the shapes fit together exactly, or tessellate. This activity explores the idea of tessellation – you could follow it up by using common household shapes, such as circular plates, square mats, etc.

Pages 16–17 When people talk to each other they pick up signals from gestures, tone of voice, and body language, as well as from the words. Exploring the ways that animals communicate with us and with each other will help your child understand this.

Pages 18–19 Children begin to make estimates based on what they see around them. They will know, for example, that older children usually run faster than younger ones. Children are also very interested in measuring their performance in sporting activities. This can reinforce basic counting and estimating skills.

Pages 20–21 This activity is about handling data. In making a simple picture graph like this, children are recording information in an attractive way. You could look for other opportunities for doing this, eg recording the family's favourite foods, or the number of different coloured cars that go down the street.

Pages 22–23 The important thing here is seeing the multiplication patterns. You can help by asking your child first to count the number of rows and then the number of panes in each row. Don't worry if they cannot do the final calculation.

Pages 24–25 Encourage your child to suggest several different things that the children could do. Understanding cause and effect, and predicting what could happen next, are important in developing higher reading skills.

Pages 26–27 This activity is about sorting and matching: important skills in science as well as in maths. Encourage your child to talk about what they're doing as they guess.

Pages 28–29 Estimating the passage of time is something that both adults and children find difficult. Saying 'one elephant, two elephants, three elephants', and so on up to ten, will help your child to recognise how long it takes for ten seconds to elapse, and will prevent them rushing through the numbers.

Pages 30–31 Writing your own adventure story is more than just fun. The comic strip format with speech bubbles also gives useful practice in writing in sentences and using punctuation.

About the authors and advisers

Irene Yates is a writer and teacher in charge of language development at Lakey Lane School in Birmingham.

David Bell is Assistant Director of Education (Forward Planning) for Newcastle upon Tyne City Council, a former primary head and maths specialist.

Geoff Leyland is Deputy Head of Deer Park Primary School in Derbyshire and a former science and technology advisory teacher.

Mick Seller is Deputy Head of Asterdale Primary School in Derbyshire and a former science and technology advisory teacher.

Elizabeth Bassant is a language advisory teacher in Haringey, London. **Peter Ovens** is Principal Lecturer for Curriculum and Professional Development at Nottingham Polytechnic and a science specialist. **Peter Patilla** is a maths consultant, author and Senior Lecturer in Mathematics Education at Sheffield Polytechnic.

Margaret Williams is an advisory teacher for maths in Newton Abbott, Devon.